First published in Great Britain in 2017
by Bryngold Books Ltd.
100 Brynau Wood, Cimla,
Neath, South Wales SA11 3YQ.

Typesetting, layout,
editing and design
by Bryngold Books

ISBN: 978-1-905900-47-3

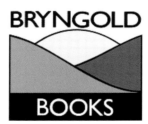

BRYNGOLD BOOKS

Printed in Wales

www.bryngoldbooks.com

Swansea

a city with
pride in the past,
the present
and the future.

About the author

Some 20 years ago David Roberts, in his employ as a journalist with the South Wales Evening Post, was tasked, as the newspaper's salute to the city, with a project to produce a book taking a pictorial look back at Swansea, its people and its places, as it bravely ventured into a new Millennium.

David Roberts

When he did so, little could he have realised that the success of Images of Swansea would see him continue to produce a similar book for each of the consecutive years in the following two decades.

Now, the publication of **Swansea — Echoes of the past,** brings to a total of 20 his personal tally of titles that take the city's citizens of today on an incredible trip back in time. No other location can lay claim to such a community album of photographs with such longevity in its pedigree. The series has been saluted as an incomparable look-back in time which captures the flavour and the feeling of the way the city once was. People, places and events all feature throughout the book's pages along with many more atmospheric glimpses of Wales' seaside city in years past.

Once again the pages of **Swansea — Echoes of the past** provide a home for a fresh and fascinating harvest of images. The book is a worthy companion for the previous titles in this long-running series and with a rapid rate of change something that Wales' seaside city is set to live with for many years to come, it will help ensure that the community will never have to look far to discover how things were.

Wheels of change

As the images in this book slowly convey those who turn its pages on an individual and often very personal trip back in time, the wheels of change are rolling Swansea into the future faster than ever.

What has gone before has contributed to a colourful history. Interesting times, interesting places populated by interesting people, have all played their part down decades and generations alike. This series of books which has gathered many thousands of photographs from a great many inhabitants of the city will no doubt assist in the keeping alive of a proud memory.

Swansea has always been a city of change. Mostly by its own volition; sometimes at the hand of those from a foreign land; always with pride and when the cry 'Who are we?' goes up, the answer will loudly be 'We are Swansea and proud of it.' The city has grasped the early years of the 21st Century with both hands. Doing so has given it the confidence to take advantage of what is promised next: a £3.4 billion bay redevelopment plan; the redevelopment of the Civic Centre and the surrounding area; the Swansea Bay tidal lagoon scheme; changes to the city centre and lots more.

The spend has never been bigger. This means the element of change that alone will thrust upon the people and places that comprise this historic city will be almost unimaginable. Just a glance at the plans of architects and the impressions of artists is enough to prove that the Swansea of tomorrow will bear scant resemblance to that of today. There has always been change and because of its dockland and maritime heritage Swansea has always had something of a cosmopolitan atmosphere. That can be seen from the pictures in this book which have been drawn from many sources. It is the 20th to appear telling an incomparable tale of the way things once were.

Swansea — Echoes of the Past offers a catalogue of images, many of which have never been previously published. This book looks at all aspects of city life and doesn't discriminate: rich and poor; young and old; photographs of the spectacular and others that some might consider mundane all join the dots to create a pictorial identikit. Many of the images in this book, like those showing Castle Gardens and the stores around it, will take the reader back to a time when for far different reasons Swansea was beginning to undergo an earlier transformation, one which many will still be familiar with. Following this came significant development of the 1970s and the decades that followed.

This book and its predecessor companion titles, combine to tell the story so far, the lead up to the exciting times that lay ahead and why Swansea will remain a proud city.

David Roberts, 2017.

A big thank you

Swansea — Echoes of the past is a book which we hope will once again bring much enjoyment to a great many people far and wide. It is the result of photographic contributions, large and small which capture some unique times from the city's past and allow it to be seen from a different perspective, often through the eyes of those who were there, camera in hand. The book's pictures are often not perfect compositions, nor the work of professionals. They are instead, the earthy efforts of ordinary happy snappers whose pictures tell it as it was and are often gems in their own right.

The appearance of **Swansea — Echoes of the past** is due in no small part to the involvement of city historian and photographer Royston Kneath, who sadly passed away before he could see his contribution in print; Julie Jones, Mrs S Rees, Bryn Wilcock, William Bateman, Barbara Griffiths, Noel Blows, Raymond & Dorothy Lewis, Hilary Evans, Gerald Thyer, Stephen Powell, Colin Andrew, Robert Wayne Davies, Steve Philips, Paul Smith, Bill Morris, Roger Evans, Gerald Lindenburn, Anthony Owens, Richard & Anne Evans, Mike Hallett, John Griffiths, Bryndon J Evans, Roger Green, Peter Muxworthy, Bill Morris, Graham Davies, Barry Jones, Irene Willis, Jennifer Pember, Stephen Miles, Miss DW Powell, Roy Morgan, Peter Bailey, Clive Cockings, David Webborn, Raymond & Rion Davies, Marilyn Hancock, Peter & Carol Nedin, Hugh Rees, Anne Howell, Roger Trollope, Roger Hayman, Alan Penhorwood, Dr Robert Howells, Roy, Colin & Eileen Payne, John & Jo Coode, Gaye Wanhill, Stuart Davies, Lisa Brown, Darren Hounsell, Matthew Burton, Elizabeth & Ashleigh Chapman and Muriel McLean.

Others without whose involvement **Swansea — Echoes of the past** would not have appeared include Charlie Wise, Neil Melbourne, David Beynon and Gerald Gabb. Lastly, but by no means least, I must thank my wife Cheryl for her unfailing support. Without that I am sure **Swansea — Echoes of the past** or indeed any of my books would never have appeared.

David Roberts

Share your pictures

If you have photographs of people, places or events in and around Swansea right up to recent times then you could play a part in the next Swansea nostalgia book.
Please telephone 01639 643961 or e-mail david.roberts@bryngoldbooks.com to discover the ways in which you can do this. All photographs, transparencies, negatives, black and white or colour, of people, places, events, streets, buildings, schooldays and sport are considered whatever their age or subject. They are all promptly returned. We can also receive your pictures electronically. Meanwhile, if you have missed any of the previous 19 books why not contact us now as some titles are still available to help complete your collection. You can also check out our many other similar titles at:

www.bryngoldbooks.com

Resurfacing work on Constitution Hill appears to have been an uphill job during May, 2004.

Swansea lost its grand pre-war market building during the ravages of the Three Nights' Blitz in wartime 1941. This view shows the temporary outdoor market that eventually sprang up in its place, seen in the mid-1950s.

Stained glass designer Howard Martin with students at the Swansea Art College Stained Glass department. Howard who died in 1972 was born in Morriston in 1907 and studied at Swansea School of Art, where he was invited to teach stained glass from about 1935. Having established a studio with his cousin Hubert Thomas before the war, the pair went on to establish the successful Celtic Studios in Swansea in the late 1940s. He continued at the College of Art while designing for the firm, becoming its vice-principal in 1962.

A single deck tramcar, No 54, operated by the Swansea Improvements and Tramways Company makes its way up Castle Bailey Street while crowds line the roadside. On the right is the renowned Ben Evans store which coincidentally is advertised on the tram. The occasion, during the 1920s, is a Band of Hope march.

Members of the 11th (Portmead) Swansea Wolf Cubs with their leaders, 1964.

A trio of English Setters and their owners are presented with their class awards after being judged at a dog show in Singleton Park during the late 1970s.

Tabernacle Chapel, Woodfield Street, Morriston stands proud above this scene which shows the back of houses in Morris Street during construction of the Morriston bypass section of the Swansea Valley expressway, 1980s.

Members of the city's Salvation Army Corps hold an open air meeting outside the parcels office of High Street railway station during the early 1950s. The return rail fare to Cardiff would be a bargain today!

A Swansea entertainment group takes a break with a refreshing cuppa at St Thomas Community Centre, 1948.

Uplands cinema in the mid-1950s. It operated in Uplands from 1913 until 1940. It is likely that a young Dylan Thomas would have enjoyed a screening or two at this particular picture house.

Members of the Swansea branch of the Cooperative Ladies Guild during a visit to West Glamorgan County Hall, early 1990s, when Councillor Vic Alexander was West Glamorgan Health Authority Chairman.

Shoppers in the busy Quadrant retail centre during the late 1990s.

The Swansea to Cork, Irish Sea ferry
Celtic Pride at Swansea Ferryport
terminal, 1992. The pilot cutter MV
Seamark is berthed behind.

A fascinating view over Eastside rooftops and the docks, 1958. The east and west piers can clearly be seen framing the mouth of the River Tawe.

Former Swansea City player Dzemal Hadziabdic makes a presentation to a delighted youngster at the club's Vetch Field, early 1980s.

Boys playing on the quayside at Weaver's Basin watch as someone dives into the water from one of two barge like vessels, Severn Side and Severn Merchant, 1957. They were coastal and river motor ships which traded to ports in the Bristol Channel and the River Severn. They were possibly loading wheat from Weaver's which, imported and distributed foreign wheat and grain to many parts.

Dunvant Scouts proudly display their certificates during an investiture ceremony that took place during a camping trip to Parc Le Breos, Parkmill, Gower, 1984.

Feeling the wind in their hair is this group of women enjoying a ride on South Wales Transport's Bristol K series open topper as it heads along Mumbles Road during the 1980s.

The site of the former Quadrant and Ravenhill Club which was demolished for road widening at what is now known as West Way, July 16, 1997.

Some of the girls who were pupils at Cwm Glas Primary School, show off their Easter bonnet creations, 1984.

Castle Square fountain and waterfall with its Amber Hiscott glass leaf sculpture and Swansea Castle ruins and the BT tower in the background, mid-1990s.

Housing at Long View Court, Clase shortly before demolition, 1998.

A group of men with their dog take a break alongside boats laid up near Southend, 1946.

Construction of the former Cooperative department store, Oxford Street, mid-1950s. At this time, way before pedestrianisation, and the advent of the Quadrant Shopping Centre, traffic could turn into Whitewalls here. The bus would then have headed for the Singleton Street bus station.

Participants in an inter-departmental football match involving teams from Swansea College of Technology, Mount Pleasant at Underhill Park, Mumbles, December 1961.

Members of the 46th (Swansea) Pathfinders Cub Scout group in Paradise Park, Townhill with certificates they gained during a Cub Scout sports day, 1983.

Brightly lit shops at Newton Road, Mumbles, Christmas, 2013.

A shooting party in Gower, 1912.

A British Road Services BMC lorry from the company's North Dock depot pressed into an unusual duty of advertising the showing of 1960s box office hit Tunes of Glory at the Plaza Cinema.

Air Cadet gliding enthusiasts at Fairwood airport, with the Land Rover used to get their craft airborne, early 1960s.

Some of the mechanics and other employees of West End garage, Gorseinon, together with vehicles they were working on, early 1950s.

Pupils and teachers at Clwyd Primary School on the last day of the summer term, July 1979.

Technicians at the BBC's Alexandra Road studio, September, 2005. Below, a close up of the control desk.

Swansea beach, and behind the wall supporting the Swansea Victoria to Shrewsbury railway line are properties in Oystermouth Road, June 4, 1965.

Motor scooters complete with an array of adornments in Plymouth Street, 2008, spark nostalgic memories of the mod era scooters that were popular some 40 years earlier.

Members and coaches of Swansea Baths Swimming Club, 1980s.

The Tawe lift bridge also known as Morfa Bridge was built in 1909 as an iron and timber bascule bridge to link the Morfa Copperworks and Upper Bank Copperworks by rail and to carry waste from Morfa to the east side of the river. The iron bridge had a water-tank under its western end, which when filled caused the main deck of the bridge to lift clear of its timber supports. It is now a fixed pipe bridge.

Constitution Hill presented an ideal opportunity for ski practice after heavy overnight snow, 2009.

Members of the drama group which met at Zoar Chapel, Dyffaty, on a rehearsal evening before one of their popular productions at the Welfare Hall, The Man Who Changed His Name by Edgar Wallace, 1939.

There seems to be an element of the Marx Brothers about this scene at a Christmas party for the children of employees of the Richard Thomas and Baldwin works at Landore, early 1950s.

Playground attractions on the beach near The Trafalgar Arch, April 20, 2013.

This group of men were all employed as mechanical and electrical foremen by Associated British Ports at Swansea Docks in the 1970s.

Mr Greening, the proprietor of Greening's Haulage Company, Gower Road, Upper Killay, proudly holds a young member of his family aloft, dwarfed by the huge tree trunks and trailer, late 1940s.

Shoppers in High Street looking south, 1985.

Two of the porters who worked at Singleton Hospital's crush hall during the 1970s.

Steam locomotive 7226 heads a train of oil tankers past Dynevor Junction, near Jersey Marine, on the former Rhondda & Swansea Bay Railway, August 27, 1959.

The Manor, Manselton, formerly a cinema, and then a bingo hall it was destroyed by fire, September 1998.

Having fun on Swansea beach, late 1950s.

Part of the
annual
Remembrance
Day parade
heads towards
the Cenotaph at
Mumbles Road,
1989.

Dunvant Junior
School football
team, 1992.

Looking towards
Mumbles Pier from
Kenilworth Place
on the West Cross
estate, mid-1960s.

A driver and one of the early buses of the Swan Motor Services Company in the 1920s. It transported Gower residents into the city until being absorbed by the United Welsh bus company in the early 1950s.

This group of smiling children were enjoying a street party held to celebrate the Coronation of Queen Elizabeth II in June 1953. They were residents of Vale of Neath Road, Port Tennant, now Fabian Way.

Queuing for bread outside
Charles Reed's bakery,
Uplands Crescent, 1945.

Castle Square under redevelopment, September 1994. This transformation of what was once the green oasis of Castle Gardens, aroused much concern among Swansea residents.

Pupils of form III South Glanmor School for Girls, September 1956.

Construction underway on new buildings at Swansea University, 1957. The shell of the physics block, later named Fulton House, can be seen, top right, with students and lecturers at the official opening between two external views.

The steam ship Brora in the South Dock basin on May 22, 1958. Built in 1924 at Troon she and her sister vessels operated a regular service carrying general coastal cargo between Glasgow, Belfast and the Bristol Channel ports. She was designed for safe, fast handling of cargo and carried a small number of passengers.

Bunting flies high over Hill Street, North Hill, when the time came to celebrate the Silver Jubilee of Queen Elizabeth II, July 1977.

Engineering and cleaning staff at the South Wales Transport Company's Brunswick Street depot, shortly before it closed in 1987.

A Wales Gas lorry loaded and ready to make a delivery of bottled gas from the company's Hafod Depot, 1970s.

Representatives of the Swansea branch of the British Red Cross during a major music event held at Singleton Park, 2000.

These youngsters took part in a concert
at Cadle Chapel, Swansea, 1954.

The paddle steamer Waverly during a visit to Swansea Ferryport.

Following the parade at St Thomas Carnival, 1958.

Pupils of the reception class at Sketty Infants' School with their teacher Mrs Judge and nursery nurse Mrs Grey, 1983.

Swansea Lord Mayor and Lady Mayoress, Councillor and Mrs Trevor Burtonshaw, attending a prize giving event at Montana Park Community Centre, 1984.

Looking down on the Quadrant bus station from the roof of the Grand Theatre, 1986.

'Pop' Evans outside his new prefab home at Llanelli Place, Foresthall, late 1940s.

Bassett's Park Garage, West End, Gorseinon, early 1950s.

Lock gate engineers employed at Swansea Docks, 1970.

Looking up Walter Road, 1920s. The absence of much traffic and the casual gait of the folk on the pavement hints that it might be a Sunday. The gentleman on the left appears to be hailing the tram.

High Street shopping arcade with Snells music shop on the left, shortly before demolition, mid-1960s.

Clown Kev, aka Kevin Johns, provides entertainment for passers by at one of Swansea's 1980s boat shows.

Looking along Dillwyn Street, late 1950s.

Blacksmith David Thomas and his mate Ronnie Payne carrying out repairs to a dredger bucket at Swansea Docks, mid-1970s.

Residents of Portia Terrace, North Hill, during the street party they held to celebrate the wedding of Prince Charles and Lady Diana, 1981.

Members of the congregation of Tabernacle Chapel, Morriston, during the mid-1960s.

Vintage excursion vessel, MV Balmoral, docks at Ilfracombe with a contingent of Swansea visitors on board, 1980s.

Looking down on the Ravenhill, Portmead and Penlan areas. In the centre is the sprawling bus depot once occupied by the South Wales Transport Company, late 1950s.

Pupils of Llangyfelach Junior School dressed as pirates during their Christmas concert, December, 2015.

One of the floats in a Mumbles carnival parade passes Western Lane, early 1950s.

A presentation of gifts for the work centre at Longfields home for the disabled, 1970s.

New Road and Bishopston viewed from Kittle mid-1920s. This wide road was built to replace the narrow, steep hill that previously plunged down behind the two walkers. The car was probably the photographer's.

All dressed up for a birthday party are these six young ladies of Llwyn Derw, Fforestfach, 1957.

Mumbles Lifeboat station, with the sweep of Swansea Bay reflected in an evening tide, 1984.

Former headmaster Harry Trew and deputy headteacher Morlais Williams with pupils of Sketty school, 1990.

The statue of Dylan Thomas stares wistfully over his shoulder from its elevated chair in the square of his name in the Maritime Quarter, 1998.

Singleton hospital, shortly after it was completed in 1968. It is a 550-bed hospital located in Sketty Lane, currently operated by Abertawe Bro Morgannwg University Health Board.

The original Mumbles Road stand of St Helen's rugby and cricket ground, 1990s.

Workmen employed by construction firm Robert M Douglas during the building of Velindre tinplate works, 1954.

Bridges that carried rail traffic near the Swansea Vale Smelter Works, Llansamlet, early 1950s. The bridges carry the Swansea to London main railway line over Nantyffin Road.

Bryngwyn Steelworks, Gorseinon in its heyday.

Pupils of Dumbarton House School, with headteacher Elmer Thomas, and their form teacher, 1953.

Looking across the River Tawe eastwards towards the docks. Disused locks gates can be seen laid up on the far riverbank, early 1980s.

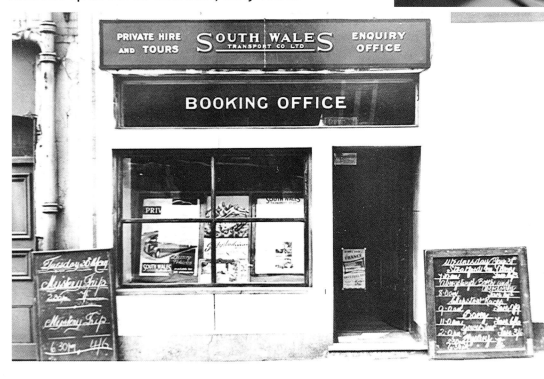

The South Wales Transport booking and enquiry office at Plymouth Street, early 1960s.

The view over the Aluminium Wire & Cable Co works, Port Tennant, September 1970. In the background are oil storage tanks and beyond, the cooling towers of BP Chemicals' Baglan Bay works.

The former Abertawe Alehouse, later Poet's Corner, March 29, 2004.

A retirement presentation for employee Les Painter in the BT tower block, the Strand, 1986.

With landlady Jackie in their midst, members of Mumbles Rangers start their annual get together at the White Rose pub in the village, before proceeding to dinner at the Pier Hotel, 1992.

A packed Vetch Field crowd cheers on Swansea Town in action during the early 1950s.

A dazzling array of lighting in the electrical department of the now closed BHS store in Oxford Street, 2015. Alongside a look through the once popular store.

The remains of The Tower, the former cinema, ballroom and bingo hall after it was destroyed by fire and its namesake, the water tower, still standing behind.

Another part of old Swansea before demolition in May 1996. Pasty's High Street café was a regular stop for the city's taxi drivers and the building on the end was popular for faggots and peas.

Singing sensation Bonnie Tyler in concert with pop group Man at the Patti Pavilion, December 2004.

Erection of the pavilion for the Royal National Eisteddfod of Wales at Singleton Park, 1964.

Pupils in their classroom at Terrace Road Primary School, Mount Pleasant, mid-1970s.

A busy summer scene along Mumbles Road, Blackpill as a South Wales Transport bus heads for the bays while a steam train crosses the road in the background heading into Swansea Victoria station, early 1950s.

Joyce and George Griffiths pose alongside the former Glynn Vivian Art Gallery garden, with a wartime entertainment group, 1940s. Behind the group is the former Workingmen's Club.

Fresh produce stalls at Swansea Market, mid-1970s.

The entrance to the former Midland Station terminus at St Thomas, mid-1960s.

A line-up of Bristol-make and AEC Regent double deck buses along with two Bristol saloons at the Upper Bank depot of former coach company Morris Brothers, early 1980s.

The premises occupied by the Swansea Plastics company was destroyed by fire and construction of a new building can be seen in progress in The Strand, October 2016.

Members of a popular Swansea wartime entertainment group at a get together, in the late 1940s. They eventually disbanded in 1951.

Staff of outfitters Sidney Heath all set for their annual coach trip, summer 1939.

Caswell Bay attracted hordes of visitors on this sunny summer day in the 1920s. Many of them had obviously arrived by car.

Crowds line the route of the royal cavalcade as it proceeds along Broadway and Townhill Road during a visit to Swansea by Queen Elizabeth II during her Silver Jubilee year, 1977.

The general hospital and immaculately manicured bowling green, Gorseinon.

The area 17 & 18 committee members of Electronics Trade Union, during a meeting they held at the Mackworth Hotel's Talbot Hall, January 4, 1950.

Members of the Swansea branch of the city's Cooperative Ladies Guild at an annual supper, late 1950s.

Holy Trinity Church, Gorseinon, in the late 1960s. It has since been demolished and replaced with housing.

An array of fire and rescue vehicles including, on the far left, the wartime 'Big Six' tender, on the forecourt of Swansea Central Fire Station, Grove Place, 1999. This is now the site of Swansea Central Police headquarters.

If you wanted an umbrella or walking stick in the Swansea of the early 1900s then this shop at 7 Portland Street, owned by Rowe & Co appears to have been the place to go.

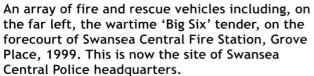

A South Wales Transport AEC Regent V double decker waits its next turn of duty from the terminus in the shadow of the Slip Bridge, April 20th, 1974. This was the last day of the old service numbers derived from the city's former tramway routes in 1937. The next day all would change.

The Watney Truman beer distribution centre, Neath Road, Plasmarl, 1976.

Brynmill Arch which allowed pedestrians to reach Swansea Sands, under the London and North Western Railway line in and out of Swansea Victoria railway station, early 1900s.

The main entrance to Pontardulais railway station, late 1950s.

Pupils of class 2B, Dynevor School, mid-1950s, shortly before the retirement of headmaster Glan Powell, who is seated in the centre front.

The Sold flash on the For Sale sign on Bill Edwards' sports shop in King Edward Road heralded the end of an era for all kinds of Swansea sportsmen and women. The shop had been a sporting institution for decades.

Some of the participants in a street party at Caemawr, Morriston, that was held to celebrate the wedding of Prince Charles and Lady Diana, July, 1981.

Members of the Hughes family at a family wedding in 1954. They were all brought up in Idris terrace, Plasmarl. They include Denzil, Leonard, Deserie, Avril, Esme, Ronald, Alonwy and Terence.

The Odeon cinema in The Kingsway. Built by the Rank Organisation on the site of the Plaza Cinema. It opened on May 17, 1967 with Julie Andrews in The Sound of Music. The seating capacity was 1,378. It was located above a supermarket and other retail units. It was split into three screens in May 1982, refurbished in 1995, but closed on December 14, 1997. It was later converted into use as bars and a nightclub; the three spaces were named Jumpin' Jacks, Time, and Envy with a total capacity of 4,000. It was closed as the Oceana nightspot around 2014 and eventually demolished in 2017.

The Seamark pilot cutter provides the background for this picture of the crew who operated her from Swansea Docks, 1970s.

Children in fancy dress at Portmead carnival, 1965.

The Carlton cinema, Oxford Street, early 1980s. It later became home to Waterstone's bookshop.

FINE FARE

FINE FARE

Properties in a quiet Masons Road, Kingsbridge, Gorseinon, late 1920s.

Members of Murton and West Cross Short Mat Bowls Clubs after a match, 2000.

The premises of jewellers and silversmiths, H. Freedman & Son, on the corner of College Street and Waterloo Street, early 1900s.

In 1919 Gower acquired a new attraction which drew people from miles around. It was the steamship Tours, still with its wartime camouflage visible, which had grounded at Deepslade Bay.

Looking across the River Tawe towards St Thomas from Swansea's west pier, during a full tide, 1907. A quiet stroll along the pier was a popular pastime for many.

Members of the Girls' Life Brigade who were based at Gendros Baptist Church, 1959.

A group of young
friends gather in
Heol Hermas,
Penlan, 1970s.

The Old Post Office, Dillwyn Road, Sketty, 1985.

Crowds of shoppers wait to cross busy High Street at the pedestrian crossing near its junction with Castle Street, College Street and Welcome Lane, one Christmastime in the 1970s.

A fascinating view over the rooftops of Swansea's Eastside, towards Mumbles, 1958. Weavers Flour Mil is an instantly recognisable landmark.

The Swansea Devil is returned to the city in 1962. The character which had originally appeared on a building opposite St Mary's Church had disappeared during redevelopment. He can now be spotted tucked away in the Quadrant Shopping Centre.

Milton Terrace, Mount Pleasant, after a heavy snowfall, 1982.

A busy scene at the former Kingsway roundabout on a Swansea Carnival Saturday, early 1970s.

A youngster makes his choice of prize at a special draw in the Cooperative store, Oxford Street, 1960s.

Employees at the Rees & Kirby fabrication works, Foundry Road, Morriston, 1965.

Demolition of properties in Singleton Street, early 1969. Part of the Quadrant Shopping Centre occupies this space now. The street running towards the camera from the centre is Nelson Street.

Properties in Castle Square, late 1980s.

A United Welsh Bristol double decker heads up Kittle Hill bound for Pennard on route 64, late 1960s.

The new RNLI lifeboat station under construction at Mumbles, February 15, 2013.

Looking along Caswell Road, Bishopston, Gower, early 1950s.

Construction underway on the western elevation of Swansea Market in Lower Union Street, 1959.

Bride Mabel Mayne with her new husband Jack Coode after their wedding at St Paul's Church, Plasmarl, June 15, 1940.

A crane at work on the east bank of the River Tawe near New Cut Bridge, during its construction, 1972.

Members of staff and managers of Macowards department store, Oxford Street, during their annual Christmas party at the Dolphin Hotel, Whitewalls, 1973.

Cubs and Scouts celebrate with their leaders and guests after the opening of a newly renovated Dunvant Scout Hall, April 1990.

Danygraig engine sheds, with one of the GWR locomotives that were especially adapted to allow them to pass under the King's Dock coal hoists, July 28, 1958.

Crowds gather at Rutland Street during celebrations of 155 years of the Mumbles Railway in 1960. Soon it would be gone from the Swansea's transport scene for good.

Cadets and officers of ATC 215
Swansea Squadron, early 1950s.

Crowds throng the banks of the
River Loughor for the annual
regatta, early 1950s.

Scouts and Guides camping in fields at Penrice, Oxwich, Gower, early 1920s.

Three members of the Lewis family of Vernon Street, Hafod, enjoying a day out at Porthcawl, 1930s.

Members of Sketty Church cricket team with two youngsters, 1924.

A BAF Herald aircraft which operated flights to Jersey, waits for its passengers to board, 1977.

A typical Eastside scene from the late 1950s. A Lambretta motor scooter, lines-full of washing and TV aerials on the rooftops.

There was a Hawaiian theme to this float which took part in Upper Killay carnival in 1974.

The Bob Hughes carpet store, Fforestfach Cross, shortly before demolition, 2012.

A train of empty coal wagons passes through the Midland Railway station at Morriston, early 1950s.

Members of Swansea West Side All Stars Comedy Band strutting their stuff during one of Morriston's highly popular and successful 1970s carnivals.

This group of Swansea people were enjoying a paddle steamer trip to Ilfracombe, mid 1930s.

Frigate HMS Arethusa, adopted by Swansea, berthed in Kings Dock during a visit to the city, 1989.

Carnival day at Morriston, the day the rains came!

Swansea Town Football Club players and officials, 1948.

An atmospheric image of Walter Road taken during a wet Sunday afternoon, mid-1960s.

Demolition underway of the former Powell Duffryn building at 9 Adelaide Street, early 2000s.

These young Swansea children were enjoying taking part in a production of Sleeping Beauty.

This replica of Sir Francis Drake's Golden Hind galleon attracted many visitors when it berthed at the South Dock alongside the Maritime and Industrial Museum.

These happy 1920s passengers had been carried to their day trip destination by a coach operated by Bassetts, of West End, Gorseinon.

The Gorsedd Circle at Singleton Park, late 1930s.

A train prepares to leave Swansea High Street Station, September, 1989.

Four British Road Services drivers alongside a lorry at the company's busy North Dock depot, early 1950s.

The busy traffic junction between Carmarthen Road, Station Road and Ravenhill Road
at Fforestfach Cross, mid-1970s.

Some of those who worked at the Cooperative Wholesale Society office, Gower Street, 1938.

Looking across the South Dock basin towards the pump house and girder bridge. In the background is the former Coast Lines warehouse that is now part of the National Waterfront Museum.

Council employees erect Swansea's main illuminated Christmas tree, November 12, 2013. The Dragon Hotel is in the background.

Members of Swansea Civil Service cricket XI, early 1970s.

Looking across the Kingsway roundabout and down into Princess Way, 1969.

Looking across the Nelson Street surface car park towards Swansea Market, early 1970s. The car park is now home to the Quadrant Shopping Centre.

A view of the Guildhall and Brangwyn Hall, from the Slip Bridge, spring 2009.

Looking under one of the railway bridges at St Thomas towards the Bridge Inn mid-1950s.

Vessels passing through the lock gates on their way into the South Dock basin, early 1960s.

Gendros Catholic Amateur Operatic
Society members during their
production of La Bella Helen, 1970s.

One of the floats of Upper Killay carnival, mid-1970s.

Two smartly turned out drivers employed by the Vanguard bus company which operated in and around Swansea and Gower stand proudly alongside their vehicles, 1948.

Civic dignitaries join with representatives of the Cooperative Ladies Guild at the floral clock which was part of their centenary celebrations, at Swansea Leisure Centre, 1983.

Girls of form 5R at Llwynybryn Girls School, summer, 1961.

Bishopston village viewed from
the top of Kittle Hill, late 1930s.

Pupils of Dunvant infants school celebrate World Children's Day, summer 1989.

Looking from the South Dock marina into the South Dock basin with the Pump House restaurant on the left, July 6, 2013.

This group of passengers was all set for a day's adventure aboard a Vanguard Motors charabanc, early 1920s.

Staff of the James drapery and millinery shop, St Helen's Road, opposite the former Swansea General Hospital, including Lena Lewis, milliner, late 1920s.

Looking across Castle Gardens towards Caer Street, 1959.

Repair work underway on the Swiss Cottage at Singleton Park, February 18, 2014. It had previously been severely damaged by fire.

A bowls match at the Dyffryn steelworks' rink, Morriston, between teams from the Richard Thomas & Baldwin's works and the Byass works, Port Talbot, 1958.

The ever popular Big Apple, Mumbles, which sold almost everything needed for a great day out at the seaside, 2007.

Some of the youngsters who attended one of the long running Swansea Hospital balls, 1964.

Part of the parade at one of the popular Upper Killay Carnivals, mid-1970s.

Adelaide Street looking towards Swansea Harbour offices, early 1960s. The building is now Morgan's Hotel and the space on the right later occupied by the South Wales Evening Post offices.

The message on the upper front of this double deck Swansea tram heading back into the city from Sketty, says it all. It reads: The best of pals must part and signals the end of the city's link with trams in 1937.

Members of Cockett Church Band of Hope group who took part in a festive pageant, Christmas 1950.

The green oasis so beloved of many Swansea people that was Castle Gardens captured on camera one summer's day in the early 1960s. Providing the backdrop is the former Boots the Chemist store that was the first of many buildings that formed the city's drive to rebuild after the ravages of Second World War bombing.

Looking from Wind Street into Castle Bailey, early 1960s.

Looking across Swansea Sands
towards West Cross, 2008.

Workers at Richard Thomas & Baldwins armaments factory, Landore, during the Second World War.

Committee members of Swansea Rugby Club during a presentation at the St Helen's ground, 1964.

The view from a pleasure craft approaching the lock gates that allow entry into the South Dock basin, 2012.

On the 1 in 45 climb out of Swansea Victoria station, locomotive 75007 heads the 12.25pm train for Shrewsbury, on April 28, 1952. This type of locomotive was only used on the route for a short period.

Edward James and Janice Davies with principal guests at their wedding at Treboeth Gospel Hall, 1970s.

Members and leaders of the 27th (Swansea) St Alban's Cub pack with a cheque for £1,000 that they had raised for the Scout Guide Appeal Fund, June 1990.

St Leger Crescent, St Thomas, 1969.

An exciting moment during the cricket match between Glamorgan and the West Indies at St Helen's Ground, July 1973.

Three young lads enjoying themselves in the sunshine at Castle Gardens, 1960.

This was the scene in 1961 before many of the buildings, including the Tivoli Cinema opposite Star Supply Stores, were demolished to make way for the Cwmbwrla road improvement scheme and the creation of Cwmbwrla roundabout.

A mixed line-up of First Cymru buses during improvement work on the Quadrant Bus Station, mid-1990s.

Woolworth's employee Margaret Bevan, a staff supervisor for many years receives a gift to mark her retirement from Bernadette Evans at a farewell event held at the Dragon Hotel, 1971.

Construction of housing at Carnglas Road, on the site of the former Tycoch Primary School, June 19, 2015.

A group of students at Swansea University College, 1931.

Mynyddbach Girls' School's senior netball team, 1964.

143

Parents and children of Western Street, Sandfields, at a VE Day celebration street party, 1945.

The beginnings of the current book circle in Clyne Gardens, during the summer of 2006. A craftsman had been employed by Swansea City Council to carve the face into the trunk of a tree using a chainsaw.

A group of girls at Oystermouth School, early 1950s.

Venture Scout Roy Hounsell, left, receiving a special award at the Brangwyn Hall for overcoming a physical disability and completing the Queen Scout award, 1969.

Walker & Turner two popular entertainers who gave many wartime performances under the name of the Two Merry Firemen, seen here in 1943.

The Waun Wen Inn before its name change to the Cherry Tree and subsequent closure, 2003.

Prince Charles outside the Pump House restaurant, in Dylan Thomas Square, during a visit to Swansea, 1996.

The dredging vessel Flat Holm moored at Swansea Docks, 1980s.

Representatives of groups which marched through Swansea as part of the Remembrance Parade, November, 2001, seen outside St Mary's Church.

The old woman who lived in a shoe was the theme for this float, one of many which took part in Portmead carnival, 1967.

Scouts and Guides pose for a picture outside the castle and farm at Oxwich, Gower, early 1950s.

The popular David Evans
department store,
Princess Way, 1963.

This group assembled on a small field behind Bath Avenue and Bath Road in Morriston, when the residents held a party to celebrate the end of the Second World war on VE Day.

Pupils involved in an educational exchange between Bishopston School and a school in Pau, South West France, on the steps of the Guildhall where they had been given a civic reception, 1985.

A South Wales Transport AEC Reliance bus begins the long climb up Mount Pleasant to Townhill in the spring of 1965.

A trawler berthed at the South Dock, 1957.

Proudly displaying the spoils of a successful season are one of the sports teams of the Collier's Arms public house, Bonymaen, mid 1950s.

Trams pass one another in High Street 1901.

Fforestfach Cross, early 1980s.

Guests at a presentation event held by the Electronics Trade Union to award its Gold Badge to Swansea Area President, Ernie Hurlestone, May 29, 1956.

Views taken during an open day at Mumbles Lighthouse, September 15, 1996.

Members of the 11th (Swansea) Portmead Scouts and one of their leaders on a float which took part in Portmead carnival, 1965.

Sketty Hall, 2016. It has stood for nearly three centuries and in that time it has undergone many changes under the direction of its various owners. Today it is a popular event venue.

Thomas Street, St Thomas, 1958. On the left is the embankment which supported the Midland Railway station terminus.

Swansea County Court staff during a celebratory night out, 1965.

Swansea Town players in action, early 1950s.

Roadworks underway at the former Kingsway underpass, with signs of work on the former Pearl Assurance building in the background, July 14 2006.

Offices of the TT Pascoe
company, York Street, 1976.

Looking down on the New Cut Bridge which carries
the main eastern traffic artery into the city over the
River Tawe, 1965. To its left a high level railway
sweeps past the Norwegian Church and Weaver's mill
to the South Dock, while to its right another leads to
the defunct line that headed up the valley.

Park Road, Gorseinon, early 1920s.

The children of Nazareth House orphanage receiving presents from the General Manager Mr Milsom and some of his colleagues from the accounts department of the South Wales Evening Post, December 1974.
The orphanage is now the Campion Gardens Residential Home.

A presentation which took place on the reopening of the Victoria Inn, Mumbles after renovations in 1987. New landlords Doug and Margaret Baker are seen with Wales and Swansea rugby player Geoff Wheel and his wife along with representatives of Welsh Brewers.

Oxford Street, thronged with shoppers, on a sunny 1960s day.

This aerial panorama taken just before the outbreak of the Second World War shows just how great an impact rail and sea-going transport had on Swansea during the preceding decades.

A class of pupils at Clwyd Primary School with their teacher
Miss Bendle, July 1979.

St Helen's Rugby and Cricket Ground August, 2005.

A tram rumbles down Temple Street, early 1900s.

These Swansea children are enjoying a birthday party in 1987.

These people took the opportunity to walk across the M4 bridge over the River Neath at Briton Ferry to raise money for charity just days before it opened to traffic, February 26, 1993.

Preserved steam locomotive Standard Class 7 number 70000, Britannia, hauls an enthusiasts special out of Swansea High Street station on November 4, 1995.

A group of newly
invested Cub
Scouts at St Peter's
Church Cockett,
home of the
46th (Swansea)
Pathfinders, 1981.

Fresh produce stallholders display their wares at Swansea Market, 1999.

Mumbles Pier and amusements, mid-1980s.

Swansea improvements and tramways company vehicle No. 33 in Oxford Street, alongside the market, 1909.

Caswell Bay with its new road, which was rebuilt in the 1920s.

Some of the regulars with Elizabeth John the landlady of the Collier's Arms, Jersey Road, Winch Wen, early 1930s. Elizabeth died in 1959.

Pupils of Cwm Glas Primary School, with their teacher and headteacher, 1966.

William and Patricia Jenkins after their wedding at St Joseph's Church, Greenhill, March 15, 1958.

A panorama of properties that made up Bishopston village, 1920s.

A peep at the back of properties in Wind-Street and a look across their rooftops towards Swansea Museum, 2000.

Residents and their children from Fforesthall enjoy the sunshine on a trip to Swansea Beach, late 1940s.

Construction and repair work underway on one of the piers at Swansea Docks, early 1960s.

The Rum Puncheon public house, Mayhill, and surrounding properties, after heavy snowfall, March 1985.

Swansea sand dredger Long Sand working on the River Tawe barrage scheme, 1987.

Looking across the former Swansea gasworks, now the site of a Tesco supermarket, from the roof of the Grand Theatre, 1986,

There are plenty of smiling faces in this Swansea family wedding group picture in 1987.

A moody, snowy day rooftop panorama of Mount Pleasant, 2010.

Affectionately known as Tea Cosy Pete, this colourful character from Swansea's past was missed by many when he passed away in February 2015. A pupil of Dynevor School in the 1960s his name was Brian Burford.

The Bay View public house at the junction of Oystermouth Road and St Helen's Road, 1999.

A vessel loads coal at one of the hoist's in King's Dock, while a second, a coastal tanker refuels it with oil.

Plough Corner, Murton presented a challenge for many South Wales Transport bus drivers on the Number 14 route to Pennard as this mid-1980s picture shows.

Pupils of Cwm Glas Primary School, Bonymaen, with their teacher, 1967.

A crowd enjoys the music at one of the popular Heineken music festivals in Singleton Park, 1993.

The Black Prince barge which operated trips on the River Tawe from the South Dock for a number of years. Seen here on July 6, 2013 it has now been replaced by a vessel named Copper Jack.

The last day of the Tesco, Kingsway supermarket, February 2000.

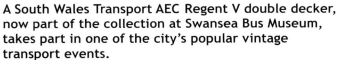

A South Wales Transport AEC Regent V double decker, now part of the collection at Swansea Bus Museum, takes part in one of the city's popular vintage transport events.

One of First Cymru's fleet of 60ft long 'bendy buses' on a service to Singleton Hospital, 2010.

A 32-seat Swan Motor Company Leyland luxury coach, 1940s.

Tyne class Mumbles lifeboat, Ethel Anne Measures which served the area from 1985 until 2006.

Members of Cockett Church
Band of Hope, 1950.

The Pullman Pub and neighbouring Espresso bar opposite High Street station, mid-1990s.

Pupils of form III South, Glanmor School for Girls, September 1956 during rehearsal for a production of the musical The Old Woman Who Lived in a Shoe.

Beach huts and the top of the shelter at Rotherslade Bay September 1993.

Two views of the subway that carried pedestrians under Quay Parade between Wind Street and Somerset Place. It was opened in 1966 and closed in 2015.

Bathers at Caswell Bay early 1950s.

Pupils of Cwm Glas Primary School, Bonymaen, with their teacher,1989.

Pupils at Llwyn y Bryn School, formerly Swansea High School for Girls, May 17, 1950.

The Quadrant and Ravenhill Club or Q & R club as it was known, the building was formerly the Swansea Castle Public House which was used by the South Wales Transport Company as a staff gathering point after the closure of the Magnet Club. This building, seen on March 25, 1990, was later demolished for road widening.

Inside Swansea Market
during renovation work on
its roof, June 27, 2015.

Children of Standard 1
at Oxford Street School
in 1928.

National Fire Service members at a gathering during the Second World War at the Guildhall, St Helen's.

Swansea West Side All Stars Comedy Band on the march and playing kazoos in a 1967 carnival parade.

A 'Bendy Bus' at Sketty Cross heading back to Ravenhill depot for the last time, August 28, 2015.